Brian Ma

BLESS THIS HOUSE

Ritual for the Blessing of the Home

VERITAS

First published 1992 by
Veritas Publications
7-8 Lower Abbey Street
Dublin 1

ISBN 1 85390 199 7

Cum Permissu
✠ Desmond Connell
Archbishop of Dublin

Censor deputatis
Patrick Jones

**British Library Cataloguing
in Publication Data.
A catalogue record for
this book is available
from the British Library.**

The author and publishers are grateful to the following for
permission to reproduce their copyright material:
Extracts from the *New Revised Standard Version* of the Bible,
copyright 1989 by the Division of Christian Education of the
National Council of Churches in Christ in the USA; A.P. Watt Ltd
on behalf of the Grail, England, for an extract from *The Psalms: A
New Translation*; extracts from the English translation of *Book of
Blessings* ©1987, International Committee on English in the
Liturgy, Inc. All rights reserved.

Cover design: Banahan McManus, Dublin
Printed in the Republic of Ireland by
Criterion Press Ltd, Dublin

Contents

INTRODUCTION

'The mission of being the primary cell of society has been given to the family by God himself. This mission will be accomplished if the family, by the mutual affection of its members and by family prayer, presents itself as a domestic sanctuary of the Church; if the whole family takes its part in the Church's liturgical worship; if, finally, it offers active hospitality, and practises justice and other good works for the benefit of all its brothers and sisters suffering from want' (*Decree on the Apostolate of Laypeople,* 11).

The blessing of a home is a memorable event in the life of a Christian family. That is why it is right to invite relatives and friends on such an occasion. It is a time for festivity, for celebration. However, the actual blessing rite may seem to be a small and disproportionate part of the occasion, so the following ritual provides a ceremonial which fits the solemnity of the occasion. It expresses the significance of the Christian home and also fosters the active participation of the family and all those present.

This ritual is intended for the blessing of a new house; the celebrant can choose whichever parts are suitable for the occasion. The celebrant may be a priest or deacon.

The rite can also be used on any major family occasion, such as a wedding anniversary or birthday celebrations, and adapted as needed.

Ritual requires more than the use of words. Each blessing may be accompanied by a symbolic action that will give depth to the meaning. In addition it will allow for greater participation by family and friends. A sample ritual action is suggested for each element of the blessing, but others may prove more suitable. These should be prepared beforehand, and be introduced by the celebrant at each place.

RITUAL FOR THE BLESSING OF THE HOME

OPENING RITE

The family and guests gather in a convenient place in the house or outside it.

Candles may be lit, and incense used.

The celebrant, vested in white stole, greets all present.

Celebrant: The grace of our Lord Jesus Christ, and the love of God, and the fellowship of the Holy Spirit be with you all.

All: **And also with you.**

Celebrant: Peace be to this house and to all who dwell in it.

All: **Thanks be to God.**

Celebrant:
Let us pray:
Almighty and eternal God,
visit this dwelling place,
and banish from it all the snares of the enemy.
Let your holy angels watch over,
cherish and protect
all who live here.
Abide with this family
and defend it from all harm.

We ask this through Christ our Lord.

All: **Amen.**

6

The following reading may now be read.
(Alternative readings: 1 Cor 12:31-13:13; Eph 5:15-20; Phil 4:4-9; 1 Jn 3:14-18)

A reading from the Letter to the Colossians   *3:12-17*

As God's chosen ones, holy and beloved, clothe yourselves with compassion, kindness, humility, meekness and patience.
Bear with one another and, if anyone has a complaint against another, forgive each other; just as the Lord has forgiven you, so you also must forgive.
Above all, clothe yourselves with love, which binds everything together in perfect harmony.
And let the peace of Christ rule in your hearts, to which indeed you were called in the one body. And be thankful.
Let the word of Christ dwell in you richly; teach and admonish one another in all wisdom; and with gratitude in your hearts sing psalms, hymns and spiritual songs to God.
And whatever you do, in word or deed, do everything in the name of the Lord Jesus, giving thanks to God the Father through him.

This is the word of the Lord.

All: **Thanks be to God**

The following psalm is now sung, or other suitable psalm or hymn.

Responsorial Psalm (Ps 99)

R We are his people, the sheep of his flock.

1.
Cry out with joy to the Lord, all the earth.
Serve the Lord with gladness.
Come before him, singing for joy. **R**

2.
Know that he, the Lord, is God.
He made us, we belong to him,
we are his people, the sheep of his flock. **R**

3.
Go within his gates, giving thanks.
Enter his courts with songs of praise.
Give thanks to him and bless his name. **R**

4.
Indeed, how good is the Lord,
eternal his merciful love.
He is faithful from age to age. **R**

Alleluia, alleluia, alleluia
How very good and pleasant it is
when kindred live together in unity!
Alleluia, alleluia, alleluia

Celebrant: The Lord be with you.
All: **And also with you.**

Celebrant: A reading from the holy gospel according to Luke.
All: **Glory to you, Lord.**

19: 1-10

Jesus entered Jericho and was passing through it. A man was there named Zacchaeus; he was a chief tax-collector and was rich. He was trying to see who Jesus was, but on account of the crowd he could not, because he was short in stature. So he ran ahead and climbed a sycamore tree to see him, because he was going to pass that way. When Jesus came to the place, he looked up and said to him, 'Zacchaeus, hurry and come down; for I must stay at your house today.' So he hurried down and was happy to welcome him. All who saw it began to grumble and said, 'He has gone to be the guest of one who is a sinner.' Zacchaeus stood there and said to the Lord, 'Look, half of my possessions, Lord, I will give to the poor; and if I have defrauded anyone of anything, I will pay back four times as much.' Then Jesus said to him, 'Today salvation has come to this house, because he too is a son of Abraham. For the Son of Man came to seek out and save the lost.'

This is the gospel of the Lord.
All: **Praise to you, Lord Jesus Christ.**

Other readings: Mark: 1:29-30; Luke 10:5-9; Luke 10: 38-42; Luke 24:28-32.

Homily

The celebrant may now speak on the meaning of the Christian home, of the domestic church, of the presence of Christ and the spirit of love.

Litany of Intercession

Celebrant: Let us now call upon God in prayer that he will bless and give peace to this house, and that all who live here may be protected from all harm.

1. That we may enjoy heavenly peace and happiness, let us pray to the Lord.

All: **Lord, have mercy.**

2. That all evil may be kept from this house, let us pray to the Lord.

All: **Lord, have mercy.**

3. That the hearts of all who live here may be open to the needs of the poor, let us pray to the Lord.

All: **Lord, have mercy.**

4. That the spirit of mutual love may ever be among the members of this family, let us pray to the Lord.

All: **Lord, have mercy.**

5. That the light of faith and the example of Christian life may shine forth from here, let us pray to the Lord.

All: **Lord, have mercy.**

6. That children may grow here in wisdom, age and grace, let us pray to the Lord.

All: **Lord, have mercy.**

7. That God may sanctify and reward the work of all who live here, let us pray to the Lord.

All: **Lord, have mercy.**

8. That God may lighten the burdens and cares of this family and be a comfort in times of difficulty, let us pray to the Lord.

All: **Lord, have mercy.**

Celebrant:
Loving God,
your Son Jesus Christ commanded his apostles to pray
that peace might come to whatever house they entered.
May salvation come to this house
as it came to the house of Zacchaeus
and may your peace ever abide with those who live here.
We ask this through Christ our Lord. **Amen.**

If circumstances allow, a hymn may now be sung.

The following may be sung to the tune 'Servant Song' or 'Stuttgart' or any other 87.87 metre tune.

> God of earth and God of heaven
> Bless and sanctify this home
> Here to you we come in worship.
> From you never more to roam.
>
> Hear our prayer, O loving Father,
> Lord eternal, ever same!
> In our midst be ever present
> As we gather in your name

All or some members of the family and friends go with the celebrant to bless different elements of the home.

Blessing of the front door

The door reminds us of the words of Christ: I am the door. Christ is the gate of salvation, through which God's grace comes to us and through which we will one day enter our heavenly home.

Ritual action: The celebrant knocks on the front door, and then opens and shuts it.

Celebrant:
Let us pray:
God our Father,
through the Incarnation of your son Jesus Christ
you have opened for us the door of our heavenly home.
Bless ✠ the doorway of this house
so that nothing harmful may enter through it
and so that it may always be open to those who come for God's sake and to those who come for help.
We ask this through Christ our Lord.

All: **Amen.**

He sprinkles the door with holy water.

The following verse of the hymn or other suitable acclamation may be sung.

> Bless the door through which we enter
> Make us free to give and share:
> May we welcome friends and needy
> And all burdens gladly share.

Blessing of the crucifix

The crucifix, which has a central place in the house, is now blessed. It is before the crucifix that family prayers will be made, and by which all are reminded of God's love for them.

Ritual action: The crucifix is hung in its place by the father or mother of the family.

Celebrant:
Let us pray:
Lord, your Son reconciled us to you
by suffering on the cross
and then returned to you in glory.
May your people who have raised this cross as a
sign of redemption
find in it protection and strength;
✠ **may they shoulder their own**
until their journey end
We ask this through Christ our Lord.

All: **Amen.**

He sprinkles the cross with holy water.
The following or other suitable acclamation may be sung.

> Jesus bore for us on Calvary
> All the weight of sin and shame:
> Bless this cross; let it remind us
> To be patient in his name.

Blessing of the Book of the Scriptures

No Christian home should be without a bible or lectionary of the Scripture readings. The word of God is a lamp for our feet to guide us in the right way. God's word is nourishment for the Christian life.

Ritual action: The enthronement of the Bible and the lighting of a candle before it.

Celebrant:
Let us pray:
O God,
you have called us out of darkness into your own wonderful light:
Bless ✠ this book which brings to us the light of your truth.
May these holy words teach us
to know you better and love you more deeply
every day of our lives.
We ask this through Christ our Lord.

All: **Amen.**

He sprinkles the book with holy water.

The following verse of the hymn or other suitable acclamation may be sung.

> Word of God that brings us meaning:
> Lamp of truth that guides our way:
> Bread of Life that feeds our spirit
> Guide our minds and hearts we pray.

Blessing of the living-room

It is in the living-room that day after day the family forges the bonds of its unity. It is here that the heart of the family beats, and it is here, too, that guests are welcomed to share the warmth of family love. It is here that the members of the family will practise charity towards each other and towards their guests.

Ritual action: The sign of peace is given in the living-room.

Celebrant:
Let us pray:
Lord God, Creator of all,
who created us to live in families
and share our joys and sorrows.
Bless ✠ this room in which this family will live.
May they find peace and relaxation here;
may they live in mutual love;
and may those who receive a welcome here
be enriched by their sharing of this family's life.
We ask this through Christ our Lord.

All: **Amen.**

He sprinkles the room with holy water.

The following verse of the hymn or other suitable acclamation may be sung.

> Gathered in the love of family,
> Welcoming our Lord in friends,
> May this room for us be blessed
> With God's peace that knows no end.

Blessing of the dining-room

A feature of our Lord's life was his time spent at meals. These were occasions of teaching and instruction with his disciples, times of reconciliation, and intervals of rest and recreation. Sharing food together spoke of the full sharing of life, of eternal life. His last supper with his apostles gave us the memorial meal of the Mass.

Ritual action: The bread is broken and blessed in the dining-room.

Celebrant:
Let us pray:
Lord our God,
you sustain all the creatures you have made
and give food to all in due season.
Bless this dining-room ✠
which brings together family and friends at one table.
May they always have food to give them strength
and love to share with one another.
We ask this through Christ our Lord.

All: **Amen.**

He sprinkles the room with holy water.

The following verse of the hymn or other suitable acclamation may be sung.

> Jesus shared bread at his table
> On the night before he died:
> Bless all those who eat together
> May their love be fortified.

Blessing of the kitchen

Christ gave us the remembrance of himself under the ordinariness of bread. God makes holy the simple things of life, and in the kitchen there is much to remind us of God. The health and strength of the family is sustained by daily food from the kitchen.

Ritual action: A selection of foods is put on display in the kitchen.

Celebrant:
Let us pray:
O God,
you have created us of spirit and flesh, of soul and body.
Bless ✠ this kitchen
in which food for the sustenance of the family is prepared.
Renewed in strength may they continue to do your will each day:
and may they never be forgetful of those who hunger and thirst.
We ask this through Christ our Lord.

All: **Amen.**

He sprinkles the kitchen with holy water.

The following verse of the hymn or other suitable acclamation may be sung.

> Martha worked to welcome Jesus:
> Mary sought the better part:
> Bless the work within this kitchen.
> Here we'll thank you with full heart.

Blessing of the younger children's room

The children's room is where they first experience love, care, protection and comfort. It is there they learn to pray, and come to wonder and reverence. Jesus loved children and his presence must be in this room.

Ritual action: A sacred image is hung in the children's room.

Celebrant:
Let us pray:
God, loving and compassionate,
your Son, Jesus Christ, came among us as a child
and grew in the care of Mary and Joseph.
Bless ✠ this room so that children may grow up here
in health, generosity, humility and love of justice.
Preserve them from all harm, may your peace be ever with them
and may their whole lives be so many songs of praise
to your holy name,
We ask this through Christ our Lord.

All: **Amen.**

He sprinkles the room with holy water.
The following verse of the hymn or other suitable acclamation
may be sung.

> Jesus, friend of little children,
> Keep them in your warm embrace.
> Help them grow in grace and wisdom
> Till in heaven they see your face.

Blessing of the older children's room

Along with the need for community, young people need privacy. Their rooms can become places of refuge from the hurts of growing up, and places of meditation on the meaning of life. The gifts of the Spirit at Confirmation are to be in this room.

Ritual action: A sacred image is hung in the children's room

Celebrant:
Let us pray:
God of mercy and compassion,
send your Spirit of love and truth
upon all who use this room.
May your blessing ✠ be upon them
in their joys and in their sorrows.
May they come to the knowledge of your
loving care for them
and remain faithful to your will.
We ask this through Christ our Lord.

All: **Amen.**

He sprinkles the room with holy water.

The following verse of the hymn or other suitable acclamation may be sung.

> Blessed Mary pondered deeply
> On the mystery of her Son:
> Bless all parents and their children,
> Make this family truly one.

Blessing of the parents' room

The priest will now bless the parents' room, which is, as it were, the sanctuary of life. Human love is deep and enduring if it is inspired by God and founded on him. By the grace of the sacrament of marriage, husband and wife share in God's own love.

Ritual action: A prayer-book or Rosary is put in the parents' room.

Celebrant:
Let us pray:
Lord God,
through the sacrament of marriage
you made woman and man participants in your divine love.
We ask you to bless ✠ this room
so that those who dwell in it may live in peace and love.
May they always remain faithful to one another
and, with their children, come to your heavenly kingdom.
We ask this through Christ our Lord.

All: **Amen.**

He sprinkles the room with holy water.

The following verse of the hymn or other suitable acclamation
may be sung.

> God created man and woman
> In his likeness made he them;
> As one flesh in love creating
> From one root the flowering stem.

Blessing of a workroom
(for manual work, sewing-room, laundryroom etc.)

The Holy Family at Nazareth lived by manual labour. Work is a sharing in God's creativity. It brings us, not only support in this life, but the reward of faithfulness in heaven.

Ritual action: The celebrant blesses the family's hands in the workroom.

Celebrant:
Let us pray:
God, creator of heaven and earth,
You have taught us the dignity of human labour
through the example of your Son Jesus Christ
and of Mary and Joseph.
Bless ✠ this room, its equipment,
and all who work in it.
May it be a place to develop the creative power given us,
and through our toil may we merit everlasting life.
We ask this through Christ our Lord.

All: **Amen.**

He sprinkles the room with holy water.

The following verse of the hymn or other suitable acclamation may be sung.

> Jesus, Mary, Joseph showed us
> How to work and how to pray;
> May our earthly labour gain us
> Harvest in th'eternal day.

Blessing of a study

Our modern world requires us to be educated in order to give of our full potential. Study is not just for those of school age, ongoing education can be a serious responsibility in many professional lives.

Ritual action: One of the family reads a short sentence from the Wisdom books of the Bible in the study.

Celebrant:
Let us pray:
God of wisdom,
bless ✠ this room
and send your Holy Spirit on all who work in it.
Deepen their knowledge of your truth;
enlighten them by your grace,
and may all they think, say or write bring you glory.
We ask this through Christ our Lord.

All: **Amen.**

He sprinkles the room with holy water.

The following verse of the hymn or other suitable acclamation may be sung.

> Wisdom, knowledge, understanding
> are the gifts your Spirit brings:
> Lead us deeper to your mystery,
> to its ever hidden springs.

Blessing of a garden/patio/terrace

This place of rest and relaxation can lift our hearts and minds to God who gives us the marvels of nature. The best things of life come freely to us, sunshine, fresh air, rainfall and the sounds of nature. We strengthen our sense of wonder and thankfulness in a garden.

Ritual action: A flower is distributed to each person present.

Celebrant:
Let us pray:
Lord, God, heavenly Father,
you cause the sun to shine and the rain to fall
on the good and bad alike.
Bless ✠ this garden (patio, terrace)
where we enjoy the wonders of your creation.
Teach us always to be thankful.
We ask this through Christ our Lord.

All: **Amen.**

He sprinkles the place with holy water.

The following verse of the hymn or other suitable acclamation may be sung.

> God who walked once in a garden
> In the cool of evening air;
> And who brought his Son to life there,
> Bless this place of rest and prayer.

Blessing of a playroom/sports room/swimming pool

Life, especially for children, is unhealthy if it is all work and no play. Jesus himself called his disciples away to a place apart in order to rest. Wise living knows how to play and work in moderation.

Ritual action: Music is played in the room.

Celebrant:
Let us pray:
Lord, we give you thanks
for easing the cares and burdens of our daily life,
and giving us rest and refreshment
when we are tired in mind and body.
Bless this room ✠
that all who meet here
may find good company,
renewal of spirit and body
and encouragement to continue doing your holy will.
We ask this through Christ our Lord.

All: **Amen.**

He sprinkles the place with holy water.

The following verse of the hymn or other suitable acclamation may be sung.

> Jesus spent his days in labour,
> Doing good and healing ill.
> And at evening rested, praying,
> By the lakeside silent, still.

Consecration of the family to the Sacred Heart of Jesus

Celebrant:

Lord Jesus Christ, by the burning love of your Sacred Heart, you revealed to St Margaret Mary your desire to rule over Christian families: behold, in order to please you, we gather before you this day, to proclaim your full sovereignty over this family.

All family members:

We consecrate to you, Jesus, King of our hearts and minds
the trials and joys,
and all the happiness of our family life.
We beg you to pour out your blessings on all its members,
present and absent, living and dead.
And may all of us,
when we have closed our eyes in holy death,
find ourselves united with you in our eternal home. **Amen.**

Ritual action: A Sacred Heart picture is enthroned after the consecration.

Final Blessing

Celebrant:
Let us pray:
Lord,
be close to your servants
who move into this home (today)
and ask for your blessing.
Be their shelter when they are at home,
their companion when they are away,
and their welcome guest when they return.
And at last receive them
into the dwelling-place you have prepared for
them in your father's house,
where you live for ever and ever.

All: **Amen.**

Celebrant:
May the peace of Christ rule in your hearts,
and may the word of Christ in all its richness dwell in us,
so that whatever we do in word and in work,
we will do in the name of the Lord.

All: **Amen**

Celebrant:
May almighty God bless you all,
the father, and the Son ✠ and the Holy Spirit.

All: **Amen**

The following verse of the hymn or other suitable acclamation may be sung.

> Honour, glory, praise be given
> To the Father and the Son,
> To the everlasting Spirit,
> While eternal ages run.

HYMN FOR THE BLESSING OF THE HOME

The preferred tune is 'Servant Song' by Richard Gillard. Copyright 1977. Scripture in Song. - Thank You Music, PO Box 75. Eastbourne, East Sussex BN23 6NW. Cf arrangement in *Hosanna,* 3: no.247, and *Irish Church Praise*. APCK/Oxford.

1. God of earth and God of heaven,
bless and sanctify this home.
Here to you we come in worship
from you never more to roam.

2. Hear our prayer, O loving Father,
Lord eternal, ever same!
In our midst be ever present
as we gather in your name

3. Bless the door through which we enter;
make us free to give and care:
May we welcome friends and needy
and all burdens gladly share.

4. Jesus bore for us on Calvary all the
weight of sin and shame:
Bless this cross; let it remind us
to be patient in his name.

5. Word of God that brings us meaning:
Lamp of truth that guides our way:
Bread of Life that feeds our spirit,
guide our minds and hearts we pray.

6. Gathered in the love of family,
welcoming our Lord in friends,
May this room for us be blessed
with God's peace that knows no end.

7. Jesus shared bread at his table;
on the night before he died:
Bless all those who eat together;
may their love be fortified.

8. Martha worked to welcome Jesus:
Mary sought the better part:
Bless the work within this kitchen
– here we'll thank you with full heart.

9. Jesus, Mary, Joseph showed us
how to work and how to pray;
May our earthly labour gain us
harvest in th'eternal day.

10.Wisdom, knowledge, understanding
are the gifts your Spirit brings:
Lead us deeper to your mystery,
to its ever hidden springs.

11. God who walked once in a garden
in the cool of evening air;
And who brought his Son to life there,
bless this place of rest and prayer.

12. Jesus, friend of little children,
keep them in your warm embrace.
Help them grow in grace and wisdom
till in heaven they see your face.

13. Blessed Mary pondered deeply
on the mystery of her Son:
Bless all parents and their children,
make this family truly one.

14. God created man and woman
in his likeness made he them;
As one flesh in love creating
from one root the flowering stem.

15. Jesus spent his days in labour,
doing good and healing ill.
And at evening rested, praying,
by the lakeside silent, still.

16. Honour, glory, praise be given;
to the Father and the Son,
to the everlasting Spirit,
while eternal ages run.

©1992 Brian Magee